Breakfast for the mind ™

Christine Michaelis

&

Nicolò Turri

Copyright © 05.05.2019
Christine Michaelis & Nicolò Turri

ISBN: 9781703348699

Win free access to the Creative Start-Up Academy Webinar Recordings

Post a picture of the book and why you like it on Instagram using the hashtag #dinnerforthemind and you can win free access to the Creative Start-Up Academy webinar recordings which also comes with monthly online co-working sessions.

Every month we will select a random winner and announce the winner on Instagram using the @creativestartupacademy Instagram account.

A bit about us and why we created this book

We both enjoy our morning readings in which we include quotes as well as other fragments from authors and ourselves that we have previously written down. However, we have found that not always all the quotes or fragments are amazing. In addition to that we saw that there is no such book for entrepreneurs and decided to take it upon ourselves to create one that we and other people will enjoy.

We both grew up in a time before the internet kicked in and enjoyed reading a book. The morning read routine has started not too long ago but we both saw the positive effects that it had on our views of our daily lives and the way we start the day.

We are sure that if you include a read into your morning routine - however short it might be - it will also support you throughout your daily challenges with yourself and the world around you as an entrepreneur.

You will see that you will use fragments from this collection along your different journeys in life at the right time.

Christine Michaelis & Nicolò Turri

Day 1

Some people see mountains where there are only hills.

Nicolò Turri

Day 2

Don't wait.
The time
will never
be just right.

Napoleon Hill

Day 3

Humans are like smartphones. They have up to 24h battery, use applications to run and need the human touch. Sometimes they also need to be switched off and restarted.

Nicolò Turri & Christine Michaelis

Day 4

There's a lot that is good in your life - don't take it for granted. Don't get so focused on the struggles that you miss the gift of today.

Joel Osteen

Day 5

Not all those who wander are lost.

J.R.R. Tolkin

Day 6

Taking time to do nothing often brings everything into perspective.

Doe Zantamata

Day 7

Sometimes the solution is just behind the corner.

Nicolò Turri

Day 8

You have power over your mind - not outside events. Realize this, and you will find strength.

Marcus Aurelius

Day 9

You create a good future by creating a good present.

Eckhart Tolle

Day 10

Looking into the starry sky, some people will focus on the darkness, others on the stars.

Nicolò Turri

Day 11

The beauty you see in me is a reflection of you.

Rumi

Day 12

He who knows all the answers has not been asked all the questions.

Confucius

Day 13

Sometimes the hardest thing is nothing at all.

Unknown

Day 14

No act of kindness however small is ever wasted.

AESOP

Day 15

Only I can change my life. No one can do it for me.

Carol Burnett

Day 16

Let today be the day you learn the grace of letting go and the power of moving on.

Steve Maraboli

Day 17

Each of us makes our own weather, determines the color of the skies in the emotional universe which we inhabit.

Fulton J. Sheen

Day 18

The future does not exist now.

Christine Michaelis

Day 19

Every day
reaches the
night, every night
reaches
the day.

Nicolò Turri

Day 20

Sometimes you need to take a break from everyone and spend time alone, to experience, appreciate and love yourself.

Robert Tew

Day 21

Live simply.
Dream big. Be
grateful. Give
love. Laugh lots.

Paulo Coelho

Day 22

We can change our lives. We can do, have and be exactly what we wish.

Tony Robbins

Day 23

An arrow can only be shot by pulling it backward. So, when life is dragging you back with difficulties, it means that it's going to launch you into something great, so just focus and keep aiming.

Dalai Lama

Day 24

Positive thinking will let you do everything better than negative thinking will.

Zig Ziglar

Day 25

The best and most beautiful things in the world cannot be seen or even touched - they must be felt with the heart.

Helen Keller

Day 26

If you can't be
yourself, you
can't be happy.

Christine Michaelis

Day 27

Sometimes beliefs can become the truth.

Nicolò Turri

Day 28

Carefully watch your thoughts, for they become your words. Manage and watch your words, for they will become your actions. Consider and judge your actions, for they have become your habits. Acknowledge and watch your habits, for they shall become your values. Understand and embrace your values, for they become your destiny.

Mahatma Gandhi

Day 29

Sometimes life can be seen like a fairytale with all that it entails: the castle, battles, the peace, the bridge, the safety nest & more.

Nicolò Turri

Day 30

Don't wait for someone to bring you flowers. Plant your own garden and decorate your own soul.

Mario Quintana

Day 31

The more you praise and celebrate your life, the more there is in life to celebrate.

Oprah Winfrey

Day 32

Two things define you. Your patience when you have nothing, your attitude when you have everything.

unknown

Day 33

We are used to think that only a few people have the gift of creativity. It is not true. We all, as humans, have this gift, but some people are able to feed it and some are limited by their education and cultural systems.

Adriano Travaglia

Day 34

Your experience of life isn't based on your life, but on what you pay attention to.

Gregg Krech

Day 35

If you don't prioritise your own life, someone else will.

Greg McKeown

Day 36

Since everything is a reflection of our minds, everything can be changed by our minds.

Buddha

Day 37

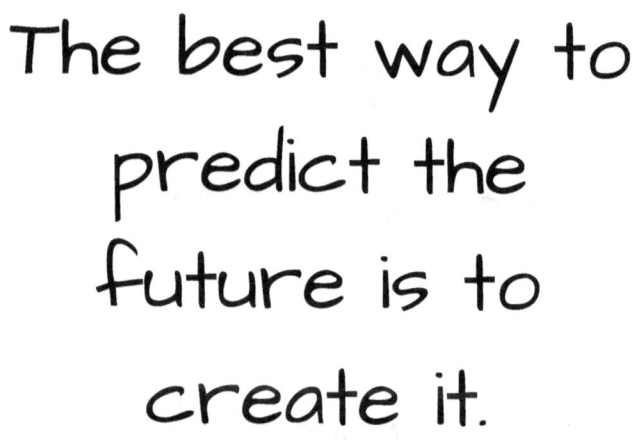

The best way to predict the future is to create it.

Peter Drucker

Day 38

The happiness of your life depends upon the quality of your thoughts.

Marcus Aurelius

Day 39

It's the little things that make the day.

Nicolò Turri

Day 40

Doing nothing from time to time is ok.

Christine Michaelis

Day 41

The simple things are also the most extraordinary things, and only the wise can see them.

Paulo Coelho

Day 42

Life and Dreams are leaves of the same book, reading them in order is living, skimming through them is dreaming.

Arthur Schopenhauer

Day 43

The beginning is half of everything.

Pythagoras

Day 44

Your mind is a flexible mirror; adjust it to see a better world.

Amit Ray

Day 45

There is nothing more beautiful than someone who goes out of their way to make life beautiful for others.

Mandy Hale

Day 46

Don't give to get. Give to inspire others to give.

Simon Sinek

Day 47

Remember, today is the tomorrow you worried about yesterday.

Dale Carnegie

Day 48

The first step is not getting you where you want to go but is getting you away from where you are.

Al. Jodorowsky

Day 49

We need to believe in the magic of the unknown, otherwise we put the events into a known pattern that we believe to control.

Nicolò Turri

Day 50

One day or day one. It's your decision.

unknown

Day 51

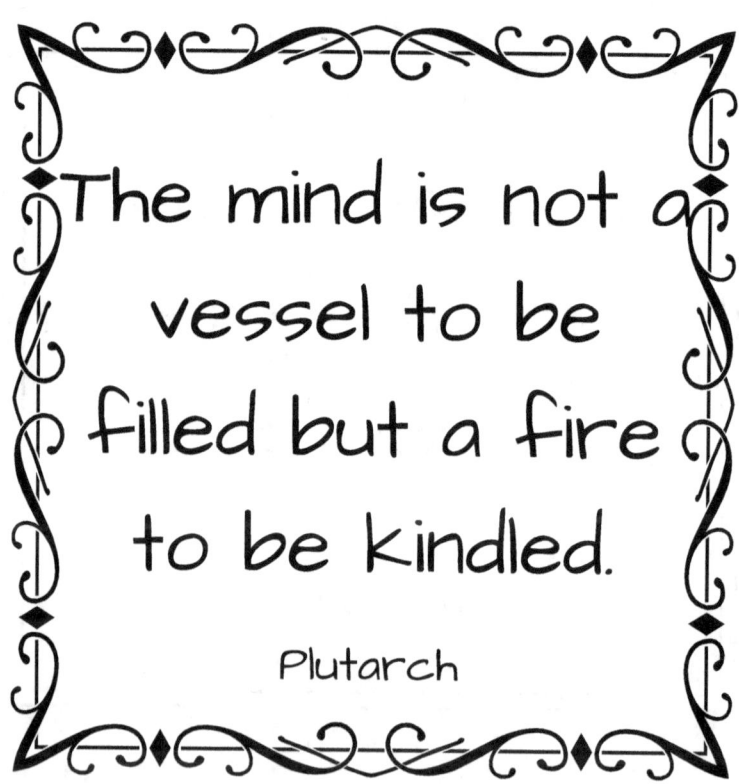

The mind is not a vessel to be filled but a fire to be kindled.

Plutarch

Day 52

Magic is believing in yourself. If you can do that, you can make anything happen.

Johann Goethe

Day 53

Falling down is not a failure. Failure comes when you stay where you have fallen.

Socrates

Day 54

Forever is
composed
of nows.

Emily Dickinson

Day 55

Those who cannot change their minds cannot change anything.

George Bernard Shaw

Day 56

Either you run
the day or the
day runs you.

Jim Rohn

Day 57

Today is
the day.

unknown

Day 58

If you don't make
peace with your
past, it will keep
showing up in
your present.

Wayne Dyer

Day 59

Give every day the chance to become the most beautiful day of your life.

Mark Twain

Day 60

Nothing is
particularly hard
if you divide it
into small jobs.

Henry Ford

Day 61

The present moment, if you think about it, is the only time there is. No matter what time it is, it is always now.

Marianne Williamson

Day 62

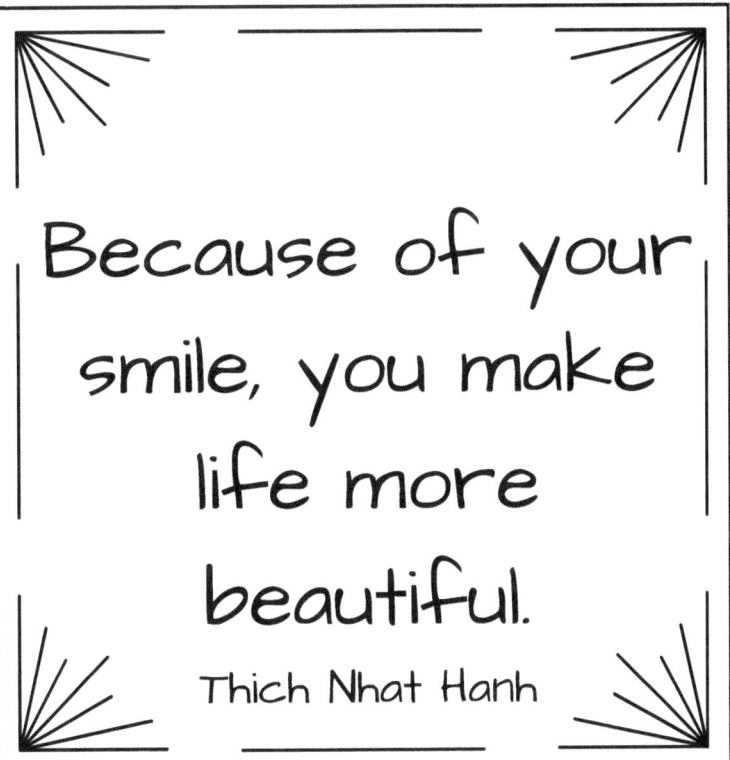

Because of your smile, you make life more beautiful.

Thich Nhat Hanh

Day 63

It's not what you look at that matters, it's what you see.

Henry David Thoreau

Day 64

The secret of change is to focus all your energy not on fighting the old but on building the new.

Socrates

Day 65

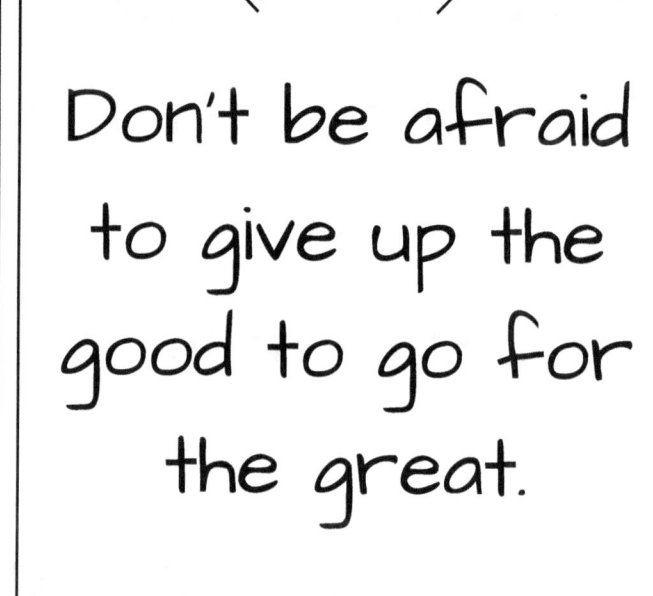

Don't be afraid to give up the good to go for the great.

John D. Rockefeller

Day 66

Each day
provides its
own gifts.

Marcus Aurelius

Day 67

Culture means to study and expand the knowledge and meaning of our cultural heritage, as innovation always starts now - not the past, not the future - now.

Adriano Travaglia

Day 68

We're so busy watching out for what's just ahead of us that we don't take time to enjoy where we are.

Bill Watterson

Day 69

Pause and remember: if you take the time to look for beauty, you will find it.

Jenni Young

Day 70

In life exist periods of
seeding, planning,
running, harvest and
resting time. It's the
circle of life. Follow
the flow without fear.

Nicolò Turri

Day 71

You want to do something? Do it! You want to learn something? Learn it! Simple.

Christine Michaelis

Day 72

Every morning
we wake up is
the first day of
our new life.

unknown

Day 73

What sets you apart can sometimes feel like a burden and it's not. A lot of the time, it's what makes you great.

Emma Stone

Day 74

> Someone is sitting in the shade today because someone planted a tree a long time ago.

Warren Buffett

Day 75

See things in the present, even if they are in the future.

Larry Ellison

Day 76

A warm
smile is the
universal language
of kindness.

William Arthur Ward

Day 77

Obstacles don't have to stop you. If you run into a wall, don't turn around and give up. Figure out how to climb it, go through it, or work around it.

Michael Jordan

Day 78

Knowing is not enough; we must apply. Willing is not enough; we must do.

Johann Wolfgang von Goethe

Day 79

Make each day
your
masterpiece.

John Wooden

Day 80

In order to succeed, we must first believe that we can.

Nikos Kazantzakis

Day 81

The true sign of
intelligence is not
knowledge,
but imagination.

Einstein

Day 82

Feelings are just visitors, let them come and go.

Mooji

Day 83

Done is better than perfect.

Sheryl Sandberg

Day 84

If not now,
when.

unknown

Day 85

Be the change
you want to see
in the world.

Gandhi

Day 86

There are always flowers for those who want to see them.

Henri Matisse

Day 87

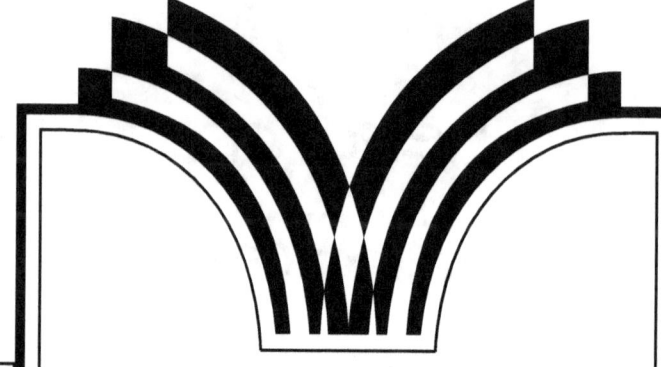

It's the little things in life.

unknown

Day 88

Collect moments, not things.

unknown

Day 89

Materialistic values cannot give us peace of mind. So we really need to focus on our inner values, our true humanity. Only this way can we have peace of mind - and more peace in our world.

Dalai Lama

Day 90

Strong people
don't put
others down.
They lift
them up.

Michael P. Watson

Day 91

Your mind is your instrument. Learn to be its master and not its slave.

Remez Sasson

Day 92

Main skills that make innovation possible are: courage, the right attitude, determination, perseverance, efficiency, and proactivity.

Adriano Travaglia

Day 93

Happiness is when
what you think,
what you say
and what you do
are in harmony.

Mahatma Gandhi

Day 94

Without the rain there would be no rainbow.

Gilbert Chesterton

Day 95

Sometimes it is necessary to eliminate adjectives.

Nicolò Turri

Day 96

What do you want from life and what have you to give in return that entitles you to it.

Napoleon Hill

Day 97

When you feel lost,
remember that you
are an example for
the others.

Nicolò Turri

Day 98

Life is 10% what happens to you and 90% how you react to it.

—Charles R. Swindoll

Day 99

When in doubt,
imagine a
wise person
giving you advice.

Nicolò Turri

Day 100

Don't let
anyone ever
dull your
sparkle.

Unknown

Day 101

Today's accomplishments were yesterday's impossibilities.

Robert H. Schuller

Day 102

Don't let
yesterday take
up too much of
today.

Will Rogers

Day 103

Adopt the pace
of nature: her
secret is
patience.

Ralph Waldo Emerson

Day 104

Be helpful. When
you see a person
without a smile.
Give them yours.

Zig Ziglar

Day 105

Freedom rings when you realise you can become what you never thought you could become.

Richie Norton

Day 106

It's simple until you make it complicated.

Jason Fried

Day 107

There is
nothing either
good or bad
but thinking
makes it so.

Shakespeare

Day 108

If you hear a voice within you say 'you cannot paint' then by all means paint, and that voice will be silenced.

Vincent Van Gogh

Day 109

The more you know yourself, the more patience you have for what you see in others.

Erik Erikson

Day 110

Tired minds produce tired thoughts.

Nicolò Turri

Day III

Don't look down
on people.
Everyone is
different and
that's what makes
life interesting.

Christine Michaelis

Day 112

Wake up with
determination.
Go to bed with
satisfaction.

unknown

Day 113

I knew that if I failed I wouldn't regret it, but I knew the one thing I might regret is not trying.

Jeff Bezos

Day 114

Life is simple.
Everything
happens for you,
not to you.

Byron Katie

Day 115

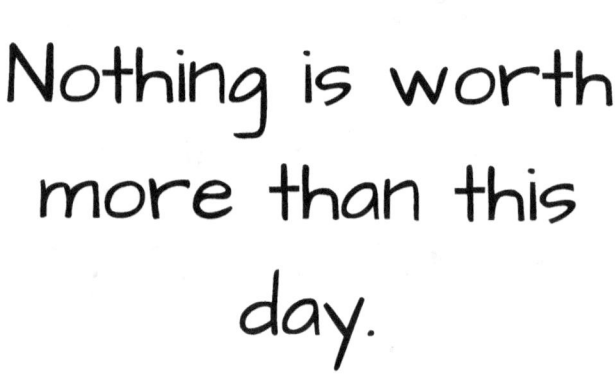

Nothing is worth more than this day.

Johann Wolfgang von Goethe

Day 116

You can speak well if your tongue can deliver the message of your heart.

John Ford

Day 117

Winning and losing isn't everything. Sometimes, the journey is just as important as the outcome.

Alex Morgan

Day 118

The road to success is dotted with many tempting parking spaces.

Will Rogers

Day 119

Change your thoughts and you change your world.

Norman Vincent

Day 120

We
are the painters
of our canvas
and directors of
our movie.

Nicolò Turri

Day 121

The most important thing is to enjoy your life - to be happy - it's all that matters.

Audrey Hepburn

Day 122

We have two lives, and the second begins when we realize we only have one.

Confucius

Day 123

Good is the
enemy of great.

Voltaire

Day 124

One may not reach the dawn by the path of the night.

Kahlil Gibran

Day 125

Be mindful of your self-talk. It's a conversation with the universe.

David James Lees

Day 126

Everything is impossible until somebody does it.

Bruce Wayne

Day 127

The darkest
nights produce
the brightest
stars.

unknown

Day 128

Little things make big days.

unknown

Day 129

A value is valuable when the value of value is valuable to oneself.

Dyananda Saraswati

Day 130

Be willing to be
uncomfortable. Be
comfortable
being uncomfortable. It
may get tough, but it's
a small price to pay
for living a dream.

Peter McWilliams

Day 131

Only the things
we judge annoy
us.

Nicolò Turri

Day 132

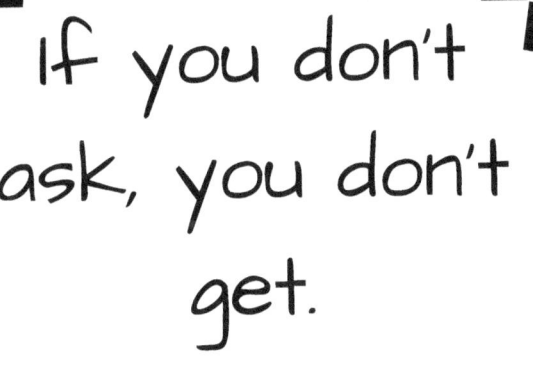

If you don't ask, you don't get.

Stevie Wonder

Day 133

Everything happens
when it needs to happen;
everyone is always
where they need to be.
You will never miss out
on what is meant for
you even if it has to
come to you in a
roundabout way.

Iyanla Vanzant

Day 134

The right person
with the right tool
can produce
great things.

Nicolò Turri

Day 135

Life moves
pretty fast. If
you don't stop and
look around once
in a while, you
could miss it.

Ferris

Day 136

There comes a time when you have to choose between turning the page and closing the book.

Josh Jameson

Day 137

If something is
important enough, or
you believe
something is important
enough, even if you
are scared, you will
keep going.

Elon Musk

Day 138

Our lives are defined by opportunities, even the ones we miss.

Benjamin Button

Day 139

He who is
content is rich.

Lao Tzu

Day 140

How we spend our days is of course how we spend our lives.

Annie Dillard

Day 141

Obstacles are those things you see when you take your eyes off the goal.

Henry Ford

Day 142

I am not a product of my circumstances. I am a product of my decisions.

Stephen R. Covey

Day 143

It's not about
ideas. It's about
making ideas
happen.

Scott Belsky

Day 144

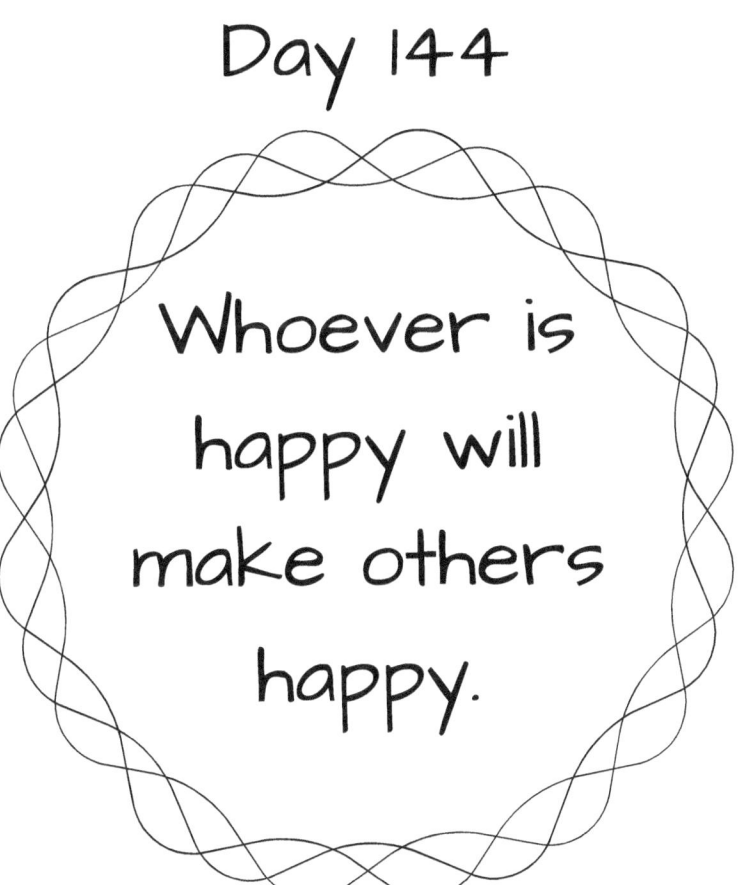

Whoever is happy will make others happy.

Anne Frank

Day 145

You can have it all. Just not all at once.

Oprah Winfrey

Day 146

Success is not final; failure is not fatal: It is the courage to continue that counts.

Winston S. Churchill

Day 147

Sometimes it is enough to exist.

Nicolò Turri

Day 148

Life is ours to be spent, not to be saved.

D. H. Lawrence

Day 149

Do what you can, with what you have, where you are.

Theodore Roosevelt

Day 150

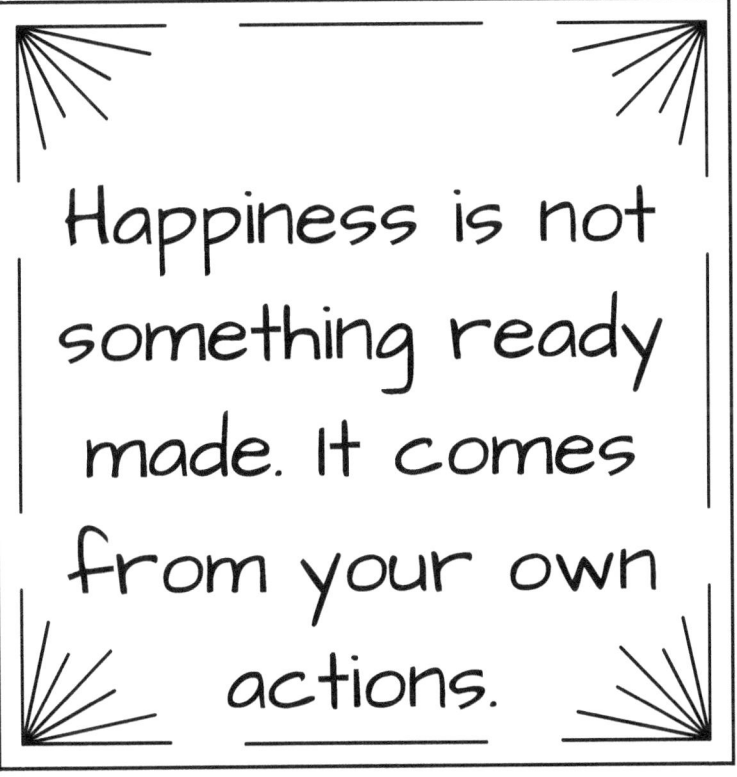

Happiness is not something ready made. It comes from your own actions.

Dalai Lama XIV

Day 151

Make time to
acknowledge your
achievements in
life.

Christine Michaelis

Day 152

Efficiency and proactivity as well as listening
to people are the only way to create relationships and cultivate them.

Adriano Travaglia

Day 153

You are never 'in'
or 'out'
of the now - you
are the now.

Jeff Foster

Day 154

We are what
we repeatedly
do.

Aristotle

Day 155

Good actions give strength to ourselves and inspire good actions in others.

Plato

Day 156

The earlier you learn
that you should focus
on what you have, and
not obsess about what
you don't have, the
happier you will be.

Amy Poehler

Day 157

Sometimes we search for something that we already have because we cannot see it.

Nicolò Turri

Day 158

Be yourself.
Everyone else is
already taken.

Oscar Wilde

Day 159

When your past calls don't answer. It has nothing new to say.

Unknown

Day 160

One of the happiest
moments in life is
when you find
the courage to let go
of what you can't
change.

unknown

Day 161

If your actions inspire others to dream more, learn more, do more and become more, you are a leader.

John Quincy Adams

Day 162

However difficult life may seem, there is always something you can do and succeed at.

Stephen Hawking

Day 163

Cherish your yesterdays, dream your tomorrows and live your todays.

Unknown

Day 164

The easiest thing in the world to be is you. The most difficult thing to be is what other people want you to be. Don't let them put you in that position.

Leo Buscaglia

Day 165

Enjoy the little things in life, for one day you may look back and realize they were the big things.

Robert Breault

Day 166

That the birds of worry and care fly over you head, this you cannot change, but that they build nests in your hair, this you can prevent.

Chinese Proverb

Day 167

Sometimes the best approach is the simplest one.

Nicolò Turri

Day 168

When we strive to become better than we are, everything around us becomes better too.

Paulo Coelho

Day 169

The donkeys prefer dry grass to gold.

Heraclitus

Day 170

Personal relationships are always the key to good business.

Lindsay Fox

Day 171

A wise man once
said nothing.

unknown

Day 172

Who teaches,
often doesn't
practice.

Nicolò Turri

Day 173

Some people dream of success, while other people get up every morning and make it happen.

Wayne Huizenga

Day 174

The pessimist sees difficulty in every opportunity. The optimist sees the opportunity in every difficulty.

Winston Churchill

Day 175

Every day can give you what the day has to give.

Nicolò Turri

Day 176

You don't have
to have all the
answers. No
one does.

Christine Michaelis

Day 177

Yesterday I was clever, so I wanted to change the world. Today I am wise, so I am changing myself.

Rumi

Day 178

Nobody can
make you feel
inferior without
your permission.

Eleanor Roosevelt

Day 179

Setting goals is the first step in turning the invisible into the visible.

Tony Robbins

Those who are quick to see their limitations generally are slow in seeing their opportunities.

Napoleon Hill

Day 181

I've missed more than 9,000 shots in my career. I've lost almost 300 games. 26 times I've been trusted to take the game winning shot and missed. I've failed over and over and over again in my life and that is why I succeed.

Michael Jordan

Day 182

If you worry about
what might be, and
wonder what might
have been, you will
ignore what is.

unknown

Day 183

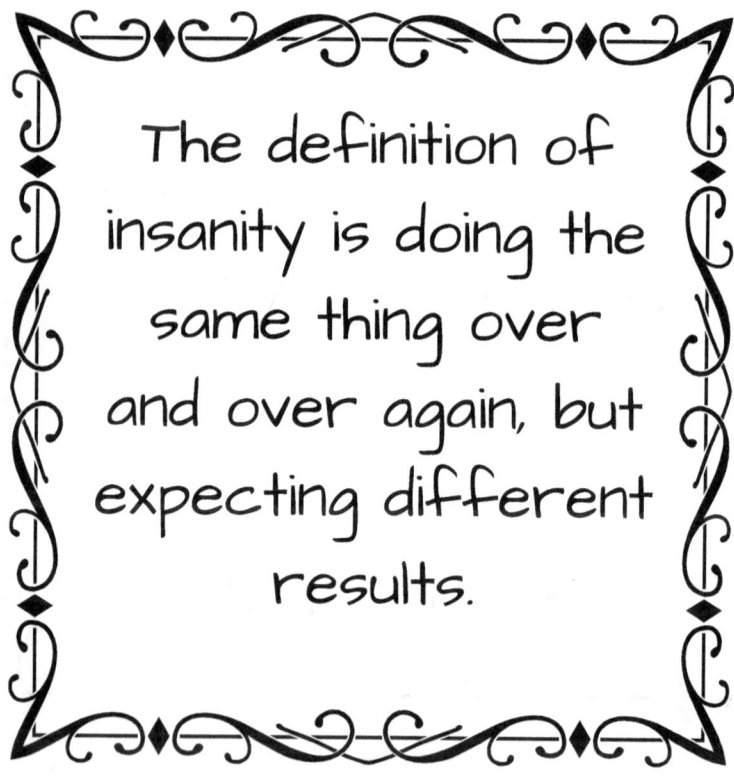

The definition of insanity is doing the same thing over and over again, but expecting different results.

Einstein

Day 184

The elevator to success is out of order. You'll have to use the stairs... one step at a time.

Joe Girard

Day 185

There are so
many beautiful
reasons to be
happy.

unknown

Day 186

The business of business is relationships; the business of life is human connection.

Robin S. Sharma

Day 187

In our journey of life we will compile lots of baggage. To be free and content, we should travel light.

Nicolò Turri

Day 188

There always
remains the
opportunity to
make a
new start.

Napoleon Hill

Day 189

Waiting for perfect is never as smart as making progress.

Seth Godin

Day 190

I have found that if you love life, life will love you back.

Arthur Rubinstein

Day 191

It's not whether you get knocked down, it's whether you get up.

Vince Lombardi

Day 192

Nothing important comes into being overnight; even grapes and figs need time to ripen. If you say that you want a fig now, I will tell you to be patient. First, you must allow the tree to flower, then put forth fruit; then you have to wait until the fruit is ripe.

Epictetus

Day 193

Somtimes you can feel unsatisfied with your work because you focus too much attention on things that actually require less energy to be done.

Nicolò Turri

Day 194

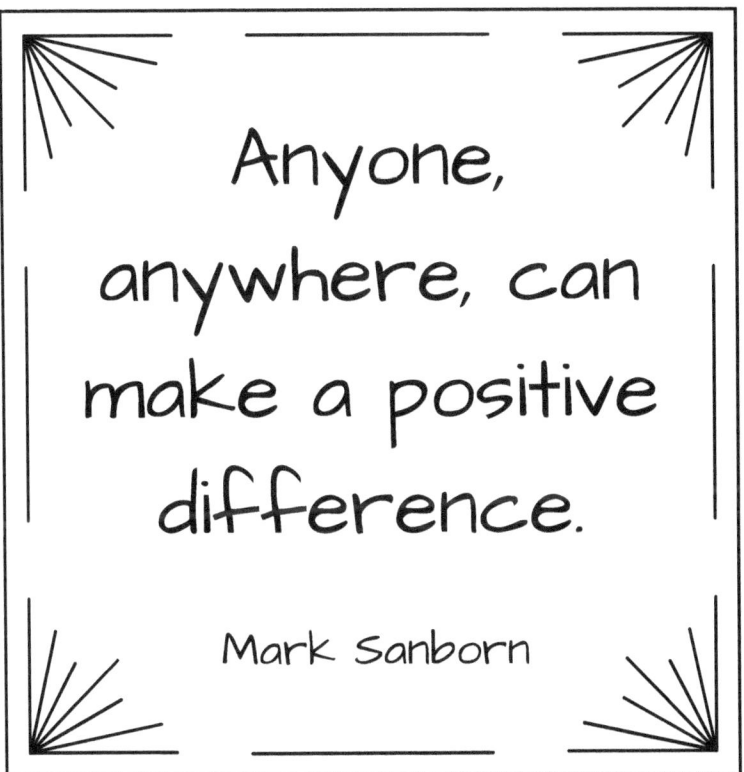

Anyone, anywhere, can make a positive difference.

Mark Sanborn

Day 195

Don't always judge your own judgement.

Nicolò Turri

Day 196

We are more often frightened than hurt; and we suffer more from imagination than from reality.

Seneca

Day 197

It is way too exhausting to please everyone. Not everyone will love what you do. As long as you do, it's ok.

Christine Michaelis

Day 198

Sometimes you
win, all the
other times you
learn.
Japanese Proverb

Day 199

Experience is not what happens to a man; it is what a man does with what happens to him.

Aldous Huxley

Day 200

The one who tries to get something for nothing generally winds up getting nothing for something.

Napoleon Hill

Day 201

Every day
may not be
good, but there's
something good
in every day.

Alice Morse Earle

Day 202

x x x x x x x x x x x x x x
x   x
x Life can only be   x
x   x
x   understood   x
x   x
x backwards; but   x
x   x
x it must be lived   x
x   x
x   forwards.   x
x   x
x   x
x x x x x x x x x x x x x x

Soren Kierkegaard

Day 203

Don't give up.
Normally it
is the last key
on the ring that
opens the door.

Paulo Coelho

Day 204

You have to create your own freedom, as it will not be given to you by default.

Nicolò Turri

Day 205

A person who never made a mistake never tried anything new.

Albert Einstein

Day 206

May the flowers remind us why the rain was so necessary.

Xan Oku

Day 207

If people like you, they'll listen to you, but if they trust you, they'll do business with you.

Zig Ziglar

Day 208

Time is the most valuable thing a man can spend.

Theophrastus

Day 209

If you really know what you want out of life, it's amazing how opportunities will come to enable you to carry them out.

John Goddard

Day 210

The only impossible journey is the one you never begin.

Tony Robbins

Day 211

The man who has confidence in himself gains the confidence of others.

Hasidic Proverb

Day 212

Keep your eyes
on the stars and
your feet on the
ground.

Theodore Roosevelt

Day 213

Listening means to understand what the other person is not saying.

Carl Rogers

Day 214

It's not about having time. It's about making time.

Unknown

Day 215

To begin, begin.

William Wordsworth

Day 216

If you don't believe it yourself, don't ask anyone else to.

Napoleon Hill

Day 217

Creativity means also making connections others people don't. So we need to enhance our ability to see connections and opportunities.

Adriano Travaglia

Day 218

There is only one way to avoid criticism: do nothing, say nothing, and be nothing.

Aristotle

Day 219

Be so good
they can't
ignore it.

Steve Martin

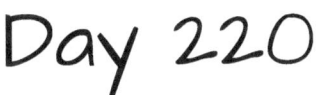
Day 220

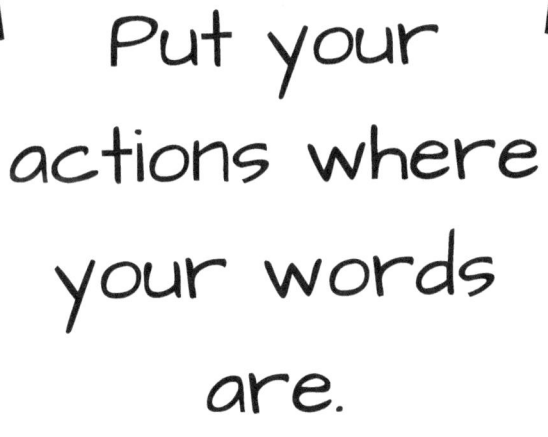
Put your
actions where
your words
are.
Christine Michaelis

Day 221

One day you will look back and realise you worried too much about things that didn't matter.

unknown

Day 222

No person has
the right to rain
on your dreams.

Marian Wright

Day 223

If we are not the creators and owners of our thoughts, who should be?

Nicolò Turri

The most common way people give up their power is by thinking they don't have any.

Alice Walker

Day 225

'Someday' is a disease that
will take your dreams
to the grave with you.
Pro and con lists are just
as bad. If it's important to
you and you want to do it
'eventually,' just do it and
correct course along the
way.

Tim Ferriss

Day 226

Turbulence is the beginning of a fruitful process of transformation.

Indra Nooyi

Day 227

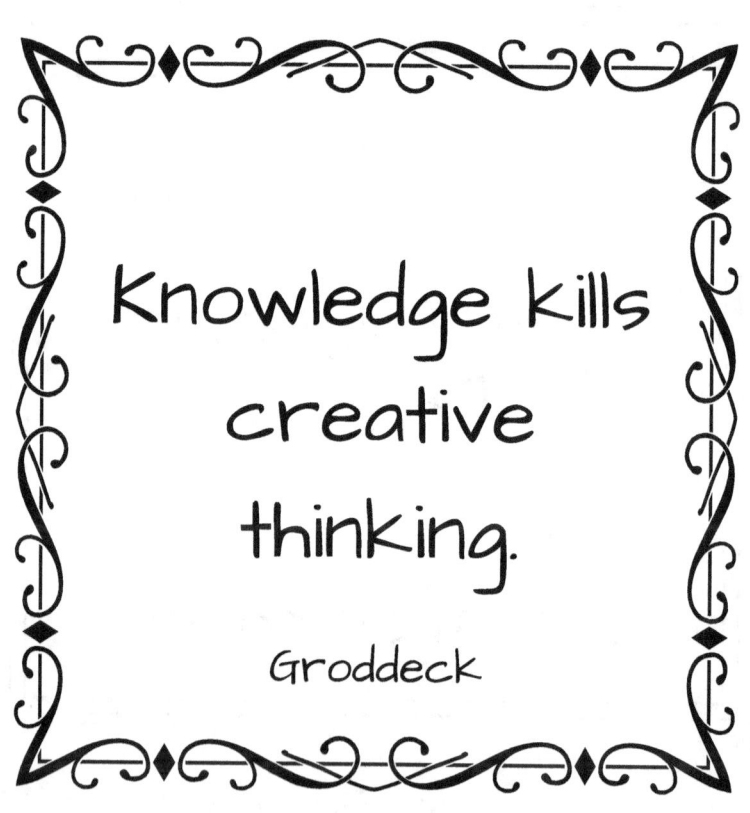

Knowledge kills creative thinking.

Groddeck

Day 228

Sometimes nothing means all, and all means nothing.

Nicolò Turri

Day 229

The question isn't who is going to let me; it's who is going to stop me.

Ayn Rand

Day 230

Someday is not a day of the week.

Janet Dailey

Day 231

Wherever life plants you, bloom with grace.

Unknown

Day 232

Become who
you are.

Friedrich Nietzsche

Day 233

Sometimes it's
ok not to
feel 100%.

Nicolò Turri

Day 234

You must learn from the mistakes of others. You can't possibly live long enough to make them all yourself.

Sam Levenson

Day 235

Dreaming, after all, is a form of planning.

Gloria Steinem

Day 236

There is a vast difference between failure and temporary defeat.

Napoleon Hill

Day 237

I always wanted to
be somebody, but
now I realise
I should have been
more specific.

Lily Tomlin

Day 238

Even doing
nothing is doing
something.

Nicolò Turri

Day 239

I have to
change to stay
the same.

Unknown

Day 240

Sometimes it looks like the biggest mistakes happen with the best intention. In the end there are no wrong decisions but just the judgement that we give to our point of view. In this way, we loose the overview of the truth.

Nicolò Turri

Day 241

Happiness is letting go
of what you think
your life is supposed
to look like and
celebrating it for
everything that it is.

Mandy Hale

Day 242

You need to know your limits to be able to push them.

Christine Michaelis

Day 243

Life is a
question and
how we live it is
our answer.

Gary Keller

Day 244

Whatever you can do or dream you can, begin it. Boldness has genius, power, and magic in it.

Johann Wolfgang von Goethe

Day 245

If you close something in a good way, something new will also open in a good way.

Proverb

Day 246

There are two types of people who will tell you that you cannot make a difference in this world: those who are afraid to try and those who are afraid you will succeed.

Ray Goforth

Day 247

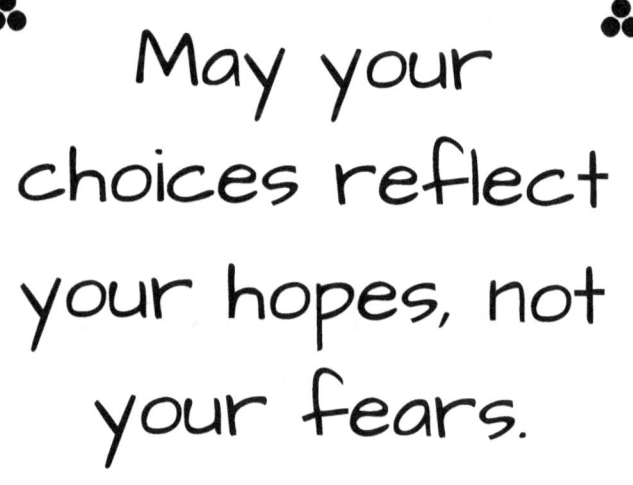

May your choices reflect your hopes, not your fears.

Nelson Mandela

Day 248

As we express our gratitude, we must never forget that the highest appreciation is not to utter words, but to live by them.

John F. Kennedy

Day 249

You're only here for a short visit. Don't hurry, don't worry. And be sure to smell the flowers along the way.

Walter Hagen

Day 250

I know of nothing more valuable, when it comes to the all-important virtue of authenticity, than simply being who you are.

Charles R. Swindoll

Day 251

Mastering others
is strength.
Mastering
yourself
is true power.

Lao Tzu

Day 252

Each morning
we are born
again. What we
do today is what
matters most.

Jack Kornfield

Day 253

You've gotta dance like there's nobody watching, Love like you'll never be hurt, Sing like there's nobody listening, And live like it's heaven on earth.

William W. Purkey

Day 254

Know what you know; know what you don't know, and be ok with it.

Christine Michaelis

Day 255

It only exists
what we want
to remember.

Nicolò Turri

Day 256

The quieter
you become,
the more you
are able to
hear.

Rumi

Day 257

Everything has its beauty, but not everyone sees its.

Confucius

Day 258

If you tell the truth, you don't have to remember anything.

Mark Twain

Day 259

The biggest challenges that we have are the ones we have with ourselves.

Nicolò Turri

Day 260

Every thought you release becomes a permanent part of your character.

Napoleon Hill

Day 261

People who are crazy enough to think they can change the world, are the ones who do.

Rob Siltanen

Day 262

Sometimes the grass looks greener on the other side but make sure you appreciate your own beautiful garden in all it's glory - the wild flowers, the bees, the people around you and everything else.

Christine Michaelis

Day 263

Fall seven times, stand up eight.

Japanese Proverb

Day 264

Trust the still, small voice that says, 'this might work and I'll try it.'

Diane Mariechild

Day 265

So, what if, instead of thinking about solving your whole life, you just think about adding additional good things. One at a time. Just let your pile of good things grow.

Susan Roane

Day 266

Believe you can
and you're
halfway there.

Theodore Roosevelt

Day 267

The most secure prisons are the ones that we build by ourselves in our minds.

Nicolò Turri

Day 268

If one does not know to which port one is sailing, no wind is favourable.

Lucius Annaeus Seheca

Day 269

Life is not always a matter of holding good cards, but sometimes, playing a poor hand well.

Jack London

Day 270

I didn't fail the test.
I just found 100
ways to do it
wrong.

Benjamin Franklin

Day 271

People often say that motivation doesn't last. Well, neither does bathing - that's why we recommend it daily.

Zig Ziglar

Day 272

Drifting without aim or purpose is the first cause of failure.

Napoleon Hill

Day 273

Whenever
you find yourself
on the side of the
majority it is time
to pause and
reflect.

Mark Twain

Day 274

Sometimes apparent misfortune can turn out to be good fortune over time.

Nicolò Turri

Day 275

There are only two days in the year that nothing can be done. One is called yesterday and the other is called tomorrow, so today is the right day to love, believe, do and mostly live.

Dalai Lama

Day 276

Some battles
are not
worth
fighting for.

Christine Michaelis

Day 277

Life isn't about finding yourself. Life is about creating yourself.

George Bernard

Day 278

A bad attitude is like a flat tire, you can't get very far until you change it.

unknown

Day 279

The art of knowing is knowing what to ignore.

Rumi

Day 280

Sometimes when you are searching for something, along the route it might turn out to be something different that you will find compared to what you were searching for.

Nicolò Turri

Day 281

I can't change the direction of the wind, but I can adjust my sails to always reach my destination.

Jimmy Dean

Day 282

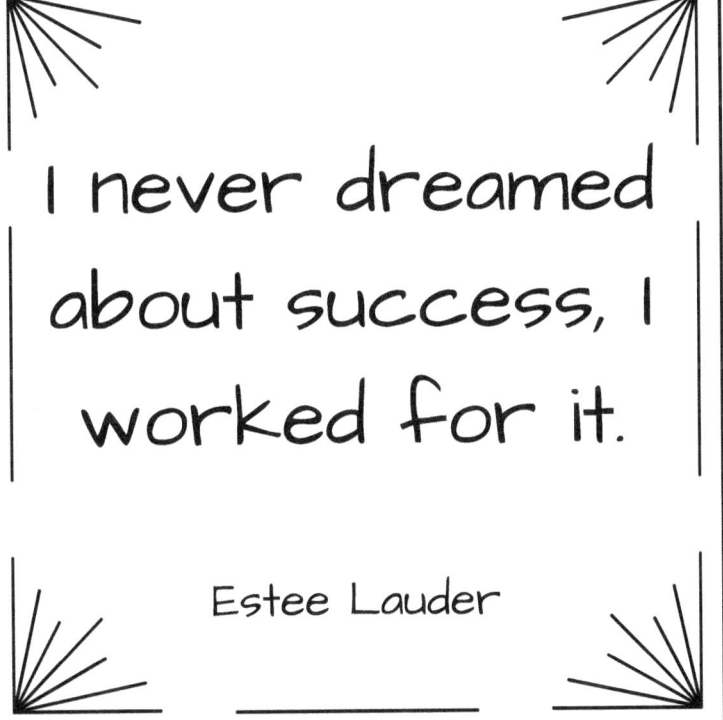

I never dreamed about success, I worked for it.

Estee Lauder

Day 283

The grass is greener where you water it.

Neil Barringham

Day 284

Innovation needs a team for the different skills required for the process. And one of the main skills of every entrepreneur is leading the team with empathy.

Adriano Travaglia

Day 285

It is our choices that show what we truly are, far more than our abilities.

Dumbledore,
Harry Potter The
chamber of secrets

Day 286

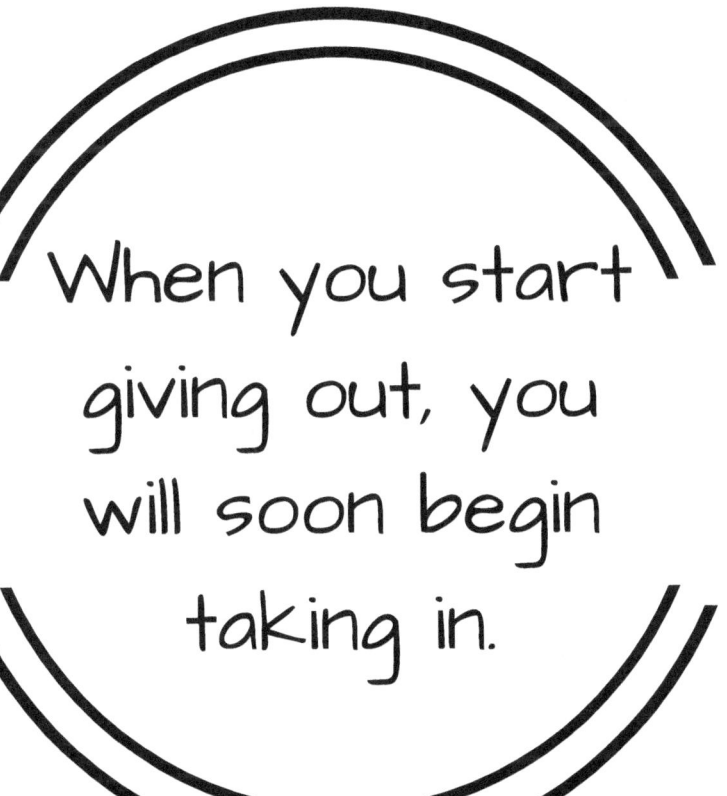

When you start giving out, you will soon begin taking in.

Napoleon Hill

Day 287

Don't be pushed
by your
problems. Be led
by your dreams.

Ralph Waldo Emerson

Day 288

In the end, it's not the years in your life that count. It's the life in your years.

Abraham Lincoln

Day 289

Sometimes before taking action, try to change your name.

Nicolò Turri

Day 290

x x x x x x x x x x x x x x
x   x
x   It does not   x
x   x
x   matter how   x
x   x
x   slowly you go as   x
x   x
x   long as you do   x
x   x
x   not stop.   x
x   x
x x x x x x x x x x x x x x

Confucius

Day 291

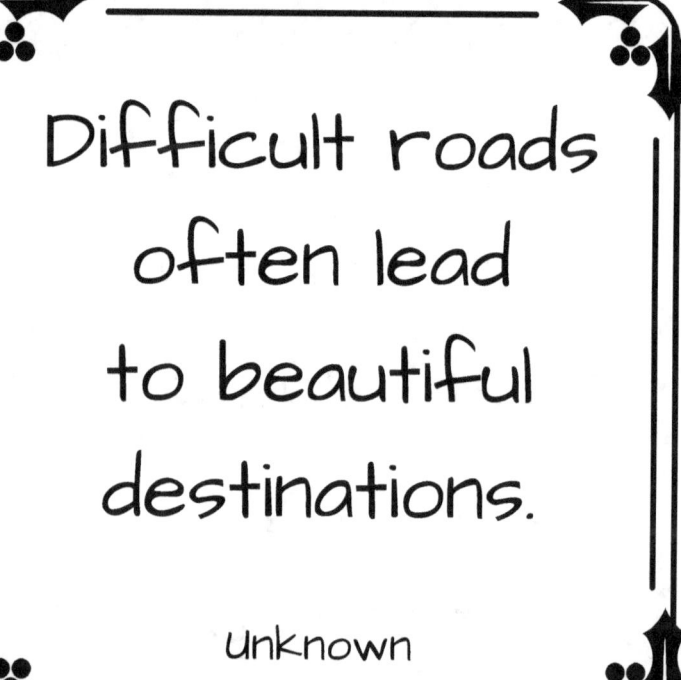

Difficult roads
often lead
to beautiful
destinations.

Unknown

Day 292

Just cause you got the monkey off your back doesn't mean the circus has left town.

George Carlin

Day 293

We live what we imagine. If we imagine the harmony of our goals, we feed the consciousness with the power that our imagination has.

Nicolò Turri

Day 294

Birds born in a cage think flying is an illness.

Alejandro Jodorowsky

Day 295

Everything will be okay in the end. If it's not okay, it's not the end.

John Lennon

Day 296

If you talk to a man in a language he understands, that goes to his head. If you talk to him in his language, that goes to his heart.

Nelson Mandela

Day 297

It is you who decides how you feel today, otherwise who will?

Nicolò Turri

Day 298

The best
views come
after the
hardest climb.

unknown

Day 299

Life isn't about waiting for the storm to pass, it's about learning to dance in the rain.

Vivian Greene

Day 300

Experience
is the hardest
kind of teacher.
It gives you the
test first and
the lesson
afterward.

Oscar Wilde

Day 301

For the person that doesn't have self-esteem, success doesn't mean anything but failure means everything.

Giorgio Nardone

Day 302

You mustn't be afraid to dream a little bigger, darling.

Eames, Inception

Day 303

There is a voice
that doesn't use
words. Listen.

Rumi

Day 304

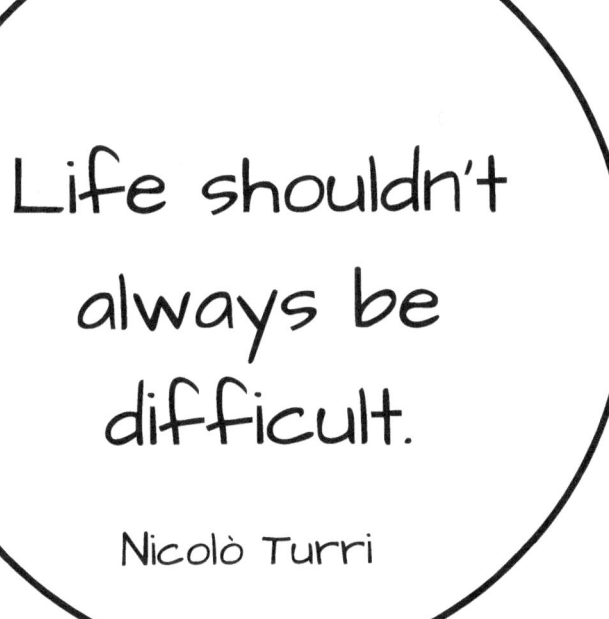

Life shouldn't always be difficult.

Nicolò Turri

Day 305

The most difficult bridges to cross are the bridges that divide words from actions.

Unknown

Day 306

Logic will get you from A to B. Imagination will take you everywhere.

Albert Einstein

Day 307

If I won't be myself, who will?

Alfred Hitchcock

Day 308

Who has time,
never has
time.

Nicolò Turri

Day 309

> Do something instead of killing time. Because time is killing you.
>
> Paulo Coelho

Day 310

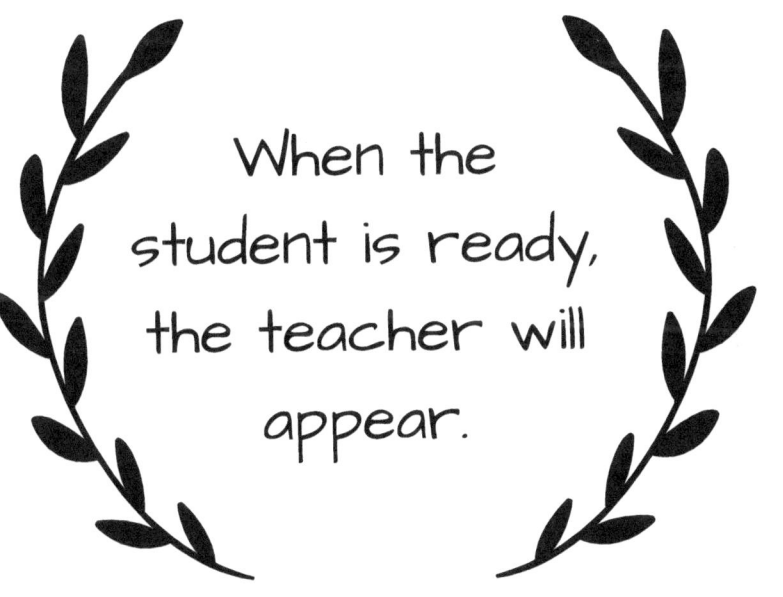

When the
student is ready,
the teacher will
appear.

Buddha Siddhartha Guatama

The difference between having and not having time, it is called interest.

unknown

Day 312

The saddest
summary
of a life contains
three descriptions:
could have, might
have, and should
have.

Louis E. Boone

Day 313

The imagination is the workshop of the soul, where are shaped all the plans for individual achievement.

Napoleon Hill

Day 314

The real voyage of discovery consists not in seeing new landscapes but in having new eyes.

Marcel Proust

Day 315

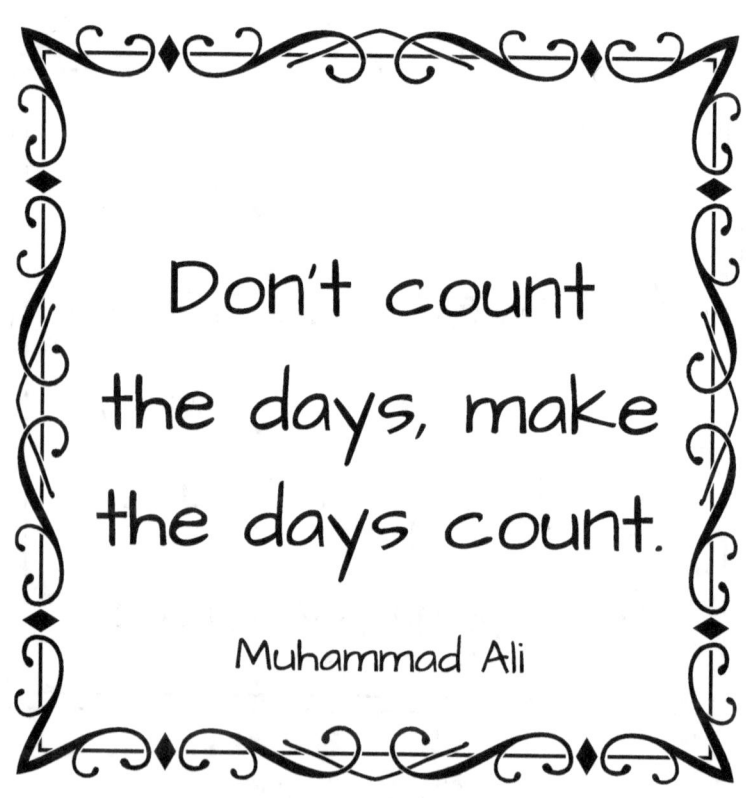

Don't count
the days, make
the days count.

Muhammad Ali

Day 316

Be who you are
and say what
you feel, because
those who mind
don't matter and
those who matter
don't mind.

Dr. Seuss

Day 317

The smell of freedom is not smelled by the nose but felt by the mind.

Nicolò Turri

Day 318

You get in life
what you have
the courage to
ask for.

Nancy D. Solomon

Day 319

A person often meets his destiny on the road he took to avoid it.

Jean de La Fontaine

Day 320

The value of an idea lies in the using of it.

Thomas Edison

Day 321

Sometimes it is helpful to change the name of the day and act as if.

Nicolò Turri

Day 322

If you want to
go fast, go
alone. If you
want to go far,
go together.

African Proverb

Day 323

Great achievement is born of a struggle.

Napoleon Hill

Day 324

Life is what happens when you're busy making other plans.

John Lennon

Day 325

If Plan A doesn't work, the alphabet has 25 more letters.

Claire Cook

Day 326

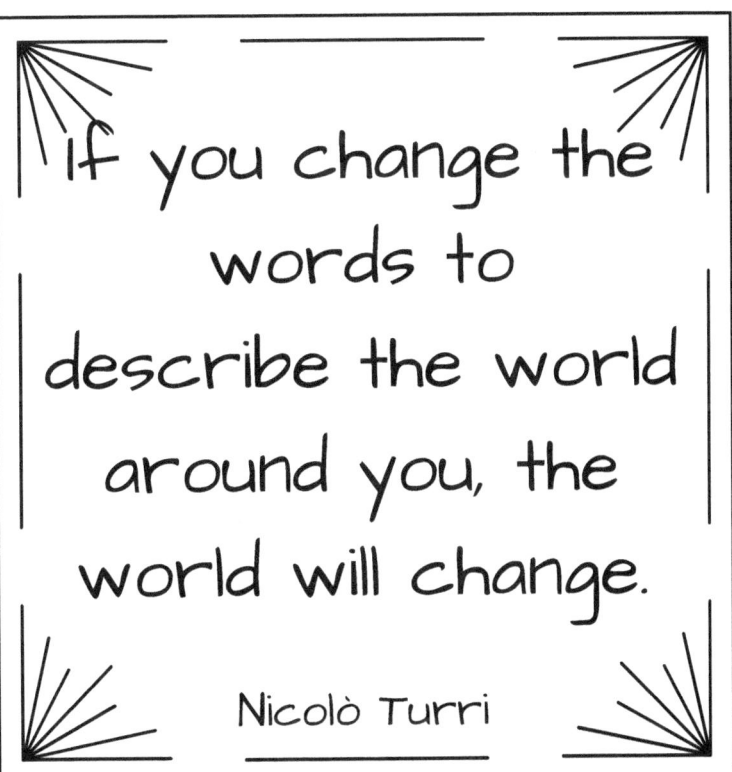

If you change the words to describe the world around you, the world will change.

Nicolò Turri

Day 327

It is ok to not know right now.

Unknown

Day 328

There always will be stones in your way. It is up to you if you build walls or bridges.

Unknown

Day 329

Confusion is a word we have invented for an order that is not yet understood.

Henry Miller

Day 330

Lost time is
never found
again.

Benjamin Franklin

Day 331

Sometimes the questions are complicated and the answers are simple.

Dr. Seuss

Day 332

Often people use a lot of energy for topics that are of no importance and little energy on real purposeful things.

Nicolò Turri

Day 333

It is not fair
to ask of
others what
you are
unwilling to do
yourself.

Eleanor Roosevelt

Day 334

New ideas are sometimes found in the most granular details of a problem where few others bother to look.

Nate Silver

Day 335

If you want to change who you are, you need to change what you do.

Repoman movie

Day 336

Efficiency is doing the thing right.
Effectiveness is doing the right thing.

Peter F. Drucker

Day 337

In the end, we
always regret
the life we
failed
to live.

Debasish Mridha

Day 338

I tell you, in this world being a little crazy
helps to keep you sane.

Zsa Zsa Gabor

Day 339

Even if it looks like you already lived through a situation, it will always be different.

Nicolò Turri

Day 340

There is only one think that makes a dream impossible to achieve: the fear of failure.

Paulo Coelho

Day 341

I do not know an infallible way to succeed, but one for a sure failure: wanting to please everyone.

Plato

Day 342

A year from now you may wish you had started today.

Karen Lamb

Day 343

If you don't like the road you're walking, start paving another one.

Dolly Parton

Day 344

Apparently there is nothing that cannot happen today.

Mark Twain

Day 345

Sometimes we feel upset if the identity if the common mentality is hurt.

Nicolò Turri

Day 346

You can discover more about a person in an hour of play than in a year of conversation.

Plato

Day 347

What we achieve inwardly will change outer reality.

Plutarch

Day 348

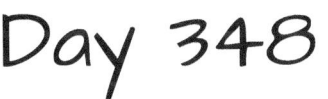

Beware the
barrenness of
a busy life.

Socrates

Day 349

What you seek
is seeking you.

Rumi

Day 350

The worst thing to approach anything is to be afraid of fear.

Nicolò Turri

Day 351

One never notices what has been done; one can only see what remains to be done.

Marie Curie

Day 352

Normality is a paved road: It's comfortable to walk, but no flowers grow on it.

Vincent Van Gogh

Day 353

Do Hard work
beats talent
when talent
doesn't work
hard.

Herb Brooks

Day 354

If we are not blind, we will be able to see the synchronicities along our path.

Nicolò Turri

Day 355

If you want something you have never had, you must be willing to do something you have never done.

Thomas Jefferson

Day 356

Tell me and I forget. Teach me and I remember. Involve me and I learn.

Benjamin Franklin

Day 357

We are not bodies that think of the soul, but souls that have a body.

Nicolò Turri

Day 358

Ordinary people
think merely of
spending time.
Great people think
of using it.

Arthur Schopenhauer

Day 359

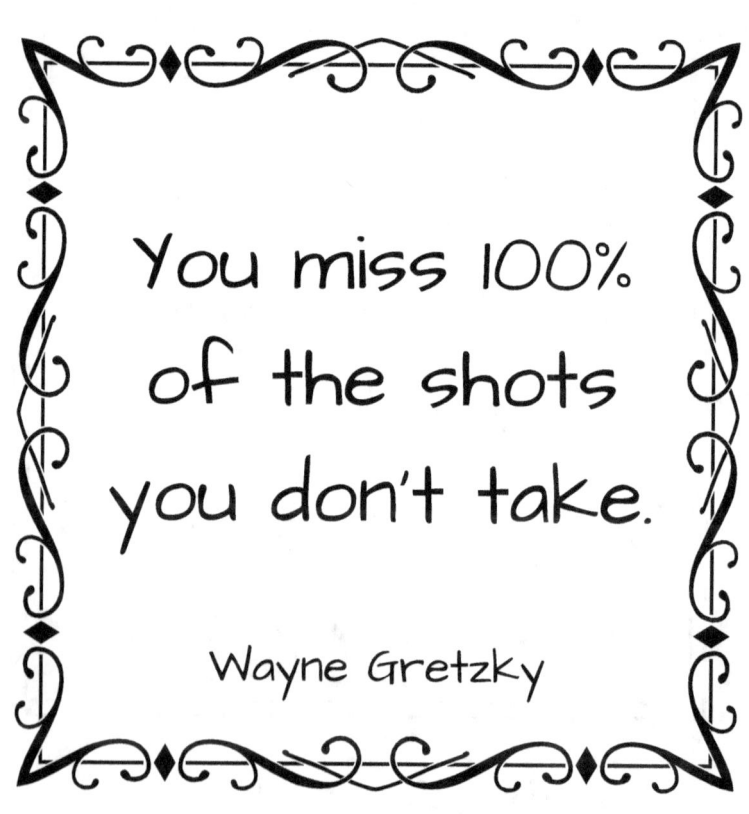

You miss 100% of the shots you don't take.

Wayne Gretzky

Day 360

Things exist only for those who see them.

Nicolò Turri

Day 361

Sometimes your circle decreases in size but increases in value.

Unknown

Day 362

It is impossible for a man to learn what he thinks he already knows.

Epictetus

Day 363

There is nothing
permanent
except change.

Heraclitus

Day 364

Everything is possible. The impossible just takes longer.

Dan Brown

Day 365

The secret of success is to do the common thing uncommonly well.

John D. Rockefeller Jr.